PETER A. BOTSIS

What is Orthodoxy?

*(a short explanation of the essence of Orthodoxy
and of the differences between the Churches)*

ATHENS

ISBN: 960-92048-9-9

Preface

The twentieth century is the century of technical development and achievement. Man has overcome many of his infirmities and reached a high point of civilization. We can say that nowadays we live in a time in which the world is united. There no longer exist remote regions where one can travel for months. We can no longer talk about East and West as in the past, as being two absolutely separate things. Today the distance between them has been annihilated; men easily become acquainted and easily communicate with people of other nationalities and religions. This fraternization and ease of communication and friendship that characterize contemporary man is without fail a hopeful sign of progress that every man approves.

In the spiritual sector, however, many lesser or greater problems arise which create questions. A great many of the foreigners (usually catholics and protestants) who visit Greece and its important monuments, among which are christian monuments (Holy Mountain, Meteora, etc.), that have been admired for centuries, have a query:

"Isn't it the same Christ Whom you and we worship? What is keeping us separate? And what is "Orthodoxy" which you so strongly and so devoutly defend?"

In the following pages we will try to give a quick but comprehensive answer to:

I) What is Orthodoxy?

II) What are the reasons for the schism between the Churches?

III) What other differences exist between the Churches that keep us separate even now?

IV) The Protestants, and

V) What are the presuppositions for a true and Godly union.

I. What is Orthodoxy?

According to saint Anastasius the Sinaite, one of the earliest fathers of the Church, "Orthodoxy is a true conception about God and creation." Orthodoxy, i.e. right belief, is the truth itself. According to the confession of Christ Himself *("I am the way, the truth, and the life"),* He is the truth incarnate. We can find and can know the truth only in the person of Christ; therefore we can be saved only in Christ.

According to the afore-said, Orthodoxy – Truth – is identified with Christ, Who is the Eternal Truth. And due to the fact that God the Trinity is the source of truth, His mode of existence is also truth, the fundamental and eternal Orthodoxy, which men have been called to follow in their own lives.

After man's fall, he lost God's Grace, i.e. he fell from communion with God, the Truth. The descendants of the first Adam, in order to restore communion with God, must come into communion with the new Adam, i.e. Christ. Man's salvation is possible only in Christ.

Orthodoxy is the holy tradition of our Church, the truth about God, man, and the world that was delivered to us by God Incarnate Himself. Orthodoxy is the right faith and right worship of God. Orthodoxy is the pure Christianity, the real Church established and preserved by Christ for the salvation of mankind.

But what is the truth that Christ offered us? And where does this truth remain unadulterated, pure, and unconfused?

The answer is found in the Holy Bible, where the Church itself is called *"the pillar and ground of the truth"* (I Tim. 3.15).

Man comes to truth, i.e. to Christ (incarnate Orthodoxy) only in His body, the Church. Man's redemption, his return to and union with God and his final salvation take place only in the Church. The Church was founded in the world because only in it can man find again his real existence and communion with God and the rest of the world. Man thus finds in the Church the meaning of life, his destiny, and moreover real communion with other men and the rest of creation. According to the apostle Paul, the Church is *"His body, the fulness of him that filleth all in all"* (Eph. 1. 23).

The salvation that Christ granted to us through His Crucifixion and Resurrection, is continued in the Church. That is why St Augustine called the Church "Christ extended into the ages". That means that **the Church is Christ,** Who, even after His Resurrection and Ascension, continues saving the world in the Holy Spirit. Humanity continuously finds God in the body of Christ, in the Church. "That is why we cannot separate Christ from the Church. There can be no Church without Christ and there can be no Christ outside the Church, i.e. there can be no truth and consequently no salvation. The truth that exists outside the body of Christ, the Church, is like gold dust in the mud. It is nothing else than sporadic beams of divine presence within the condition of fallen man and his inability to rise and be saved»[1]

Christ as entire truth – Orthodoxy – leads us to our salvation through His Church. Therefore, the Church is the foundation of the truth. If one wants to know Christ authentically, in His catholicity and fulness, one must necessarily resort to the Church. "Outside the Church, even in the so-called "christian" heresies, the inability of finding the whole Christ excludes the possibility of salvation."[2] The utterance, therefore, of saint Cyprian, the bishop of Carthage, that "outside the Church there is no salvation," is not an exaggeration. "Without the Church we cannot know Christ. Likewise, without the Church we cannot understand the Holy Scriptures, that is her Bible, her own possession and tradition. But it is also true that, in order to know Christ in the Church, the Church existing here and now must express the true Christ in His fulness. Otherwise the true Christ remains unknown and inaccessible and man remains outside salvation, which is the exact condition found in the various heresies. Only in the true Church man authentically meets Christ and is saved."[3]

The Church, according to one of the holy Fathers, is "the gathering of the orthodox people." It is impossible to think of the Church without Orthodoxy; and within this framework we can understand the Church as tradition, which is a divine

---

1. G.Metallinos. "What is Orthodoxy?", p. 19.
2. G. Metallinos, Ibid, p. 19.
3. G. Metallinos, Ibid, p. 19.

process and dynamic movement of God in History. The Romanian theologian Dmitri Staniloae says that, "Orthodoxy is a living condition, the ceaseless life of the Church."

"The Church always considered it her highest responsibility and obligation to maintain, in the Holy Spirit, the apostolic faith unadulterated and unfalsified. If the Church had not remained faithful to the truth of her existence, she could not have remained faithful to herself and retained her identity. The contents and the substance of the Church is Orthodoxy."[4]

This responsibility of the Church to maintain the truth through tradition is not something abstract. The Church takes care that each of her children remains in the truth, in "orthodoxy" and "orthopraxis" (right-believing and right-doing).

"Every christian whithin the Church must not only simply believe, but believe in one God; not only believe in a supreme and invisible power, but in God the Trinity, Who revealed Himself in Christ. Likewise, he must not simply love, but love his God by loving his fellow man. The Church is obliged to maintain this orthodoxy of faith and life and to communicate it to the world through her mission and witness."[5]

Having the above in mind, we can easily understand why the Church rejected all those who tried to falsify or refused to accept the truth of the Church, those who tried to add to or omit something from the Truth, which is Christ Himself. The Church rejected them as heretics not because she lacked love for men, but, on the contrary, because of excessive love for them, for outside the Church, far off the truth, there is no salvation. The Church cannot compromise or sacrifice the truth and the orthodox faith, because she will lose her identity and

---

4. G. Metallinos, Ibid, p. 19.
5. G. Metallinos, Ibid, p. 20-21.

catholicity. "The christian of every age must accept everything that Christ revealed and that His body (the Church) delivers. He must accept the whole truth and not a "minimum" of it. The catholicity and orthodoxy of the Church are preserved only in the fulness and wholeness of faith. The Church is catholic inasmuch as it is orthodox, because only then does she preserve the fulness of the truth in Christ."[6]

The church of All Saints (monastery of Varlaam, Meteora)

Nowadays, of course, we are used to simplifying things and to being indifferent to the Truth of the Church. Being superficial and frivolous, we give attention to outer forms and we claim that it is enough if there is a common acceptance of a basic faith, and everything more is useless. Doctrines and

6. G. Metallinos, Ibid, p. 21.

canons are made by men and they must be put aside "for love's sake."

"Doctrines, however, as rules of faith do not destroy the unity of the Truth. They create the boundaries of Orthodoxy, of the Church, so that the Church, as Orthodoxy, can be distinguished from heresy... For the Church, the foundation of faith is one: the fulness of truth in Christ."[7]

For the Church, therefore, one thing is needful: to retain the truth unadulterated, as she received it. For this purpose the Church mobilized all her powers to fight against heresy, which was her most threatening enemy. The persecutions never threatened the Church's unity or maintenance of the truth. On the contrary, they sometimes helped her gather her powers. However, heresy many times caused her trouble. For heresy, which is nought but removal from the truth, threatens the Church's own hypostasis and existence, it threatens the Truth, by threatening to sever the Truth and to divide Christ. But a Christ Who is not entire and undivided, Who is not the whole, "incarnate truth", is not the Christ that saves. Heretics did not reject the whole truth, they did not refuse Christ, but they did not accept Him entire, but only a part of Him. Arius e.g., did not refuse Christ's humanity but he refused His divinity. Others accepted His divinity and refused His humanity. But none of them accepted Christ entire and undivided.

"The truth of the Church is a fullness, a unity that must always remain undivided and unsevered. Heresy, however, tries to subject the truth of the ecclesiastical tradition to he criteria of fallen man. For the heretic renders himself judge and criterion of the revealed truth. For this reason, most heretics of every era are rationalists. A heretic (who becomes a heretic because previously he has been affected by pride, that fills him

---

7. G. Metallinos, Ibid, p. 21.

with confidence in his own reason and thought) cuts himself off from the life-giving, Divine Grace and attempts to be saved by his own power, by his own self-made "truth", not by the God-given Truth. Heresy unavoidably leads to a humanistic religiousness."[8]

So, the struggle of all the holy Fathers against the different heresies aimed at retaining the truth completely – which is an indispensable presupposition for salvation – in order to keep every man in the Ark of the Church, which is the Body of Christ. We could say that this struggle is their greatest offering to the Church. That is why they never consented to co-exist with heretics in a "minimum" of faith and to be satisfied with holding a part of the truth, but they struggled to keep it whole and undivided, for only then could they stay within Truth and obtain their salvation. The method, nowadays, in which differences are not mentioned and common points are emphasized, was never accepted by the Fathers as a starting-point for theological disputes with heretics. On the contrary, they constituted Oecumenical Synods and they struggled not for a "minimum" of faith, not to find out what is common between them and the heretics, but rather to mark out what separates, what teachings of the heretics sever the truth and, consequently, the unity of faith. Otherwise, if the Church were indifferent to retaining the faith and the tradition, as she received them, pure and unadulterated, then it would not be the Church of Christ, His Body, but a human organization or a political ideology, striving for political or humanistic purposes, and not in anyway related to Christ, His sacrifice on the Cross, and to salvation.

---

8. G.Metallinos, Ibid, p. 23.

II. What are the reasons for the schism between the churches?

Havins the aforesaid in mind, we can easily understand why the Fathers of the Church reacted so strongly and decisively against every effort of the heretics to add to or subtract from the doctrines of the orthodox faith.

It is true that during the first eight centuries the Churches were united in East and West, and together they fought the various heresies. The bishops of whatever rank (popes, patriarchs, metropolitans etc.) were responsible for governing their respective flocks and each Church was self-governed and self-administered. Whenever a question of greater significance, as the fight against heresies, arose, they summoned a local or Oecumenical Synod so that the Church catholic could decide what to do. Never in the history of the Church had a bishop, of whatever administrative grade, decided to introduce something new, unless the Church, in the form of a local or Oecumenical Synod, had expressed her opinion about it. All the Fathers of the Church humbly obeyed the decrees of the Church which, as the apostle Paul says, is *"the pillar and ground of the truth."* No single man had the right to speak on behalf of the Church or to express her truth.

For the tradition of Church, the synodal function is an essential element of its existence. It is founded on the "synod" or meeting of both natures in the single person of Christ, as theologized by the ecumenical council of Chalcedon. A fundamental synodal axiom is "let the opinion of the majority prevail". Moreover, the Lord Himself asserted that He is found *"wherever two or three are gathered in My name"*, thus implying the synodal function and the society of love. This synodical system was especially proven in a manifest manner through the Council of the Apostles, as shown afterwards.

This ancient and apostolic order, along with the unity of the Church, was interrupted during the ninth century when the Western Church, claiming privileges never given to her by the Apostolic church, showed the first signs of her love for primacy. Later, due to this love for primacy, the Western Church was lead into other dogmatic errors, which, eventually, undermined the foundation of unity and caused the later schism between the Churches which still keeps christians separated. In this chapter we will try to describe, as objectively as possible, the two principal reasons for the schism in the ninth century, resulting in the mutual anathemas by the Churches in 1054.*

1. THE PRIMACY OF THE POPE

We have mentioned that every local Church was self-governing and responsible for her region. The Church catholic never granted rights to a bishop of a larger province to interfere

---

* We must stress here that, in essence, behind the schism and the persons having played a principal role therein, there are in fact two different traditions. Such traditions finally shaped theologies that were quite different between them.

The theology of the Eastern Church was characterized by its persistence on the unity of theory and practice, of earthly and transcendental elements. This attitude is rooted in the Bible and is perfectly expressed in the dogma of the council of Chalcedon (451). The Orthodox Church based its theology on the dogma of the two natures being united in the single person of Christ. Within the Church, the divine and the human nature converge into an inseparable and undivided union, without any confusion between created and uncreated elements. Orthodoxy has always tried to remain faithful to this principle.

In the 14th century, a major theological question arose between the Eastern and the Western Church. A dialogue was held with representatives of the Western Church, in particular with the scholastic Uniate monk Barlaam the Calabrian, which impelled St. Gregory Palamas to defend the orthodox theology of the Fathers with respect to the uncreated energies of God. More specifically, Barlaam, following the teachings of Thomas Aquinas, claimed that there is no distinction between the divine essence and the energies of God but there exists a created grace and a created divine light, namely a supernatural created element.

Thomas Aquinas, who is the leading representative of scholasticism, esteemed tremendously Aristotle, as all the westerners did at that time. Thomas relied on the texts of both Aristotle and Augustine to support the opinion that the uncreated energies of God are identified with His uncreated essence. By adopting this erroneous view on the created energies of God, Thomas presents us with an inaccessible God living serenely in His bliss while people communicate with Him only through His created energies. Thus, we conclude that the gifts of God such as love, divine grace, peace, etc. are created energies of God.

According to eastern orthodox theology, the divine energies are but the external manifestation of God and constitute the basis of mankind's deification (theosis). Scholastic western theology rejects man's deification, that is, that man can participate in the divine nature by the grace of God, which was and still is the main pursuit of any striving Christian. In essence, this theology sets a barrier between

in the matters of another Church. The only thing that the Church recognized was the primacy of honor, as to who would sit or be mentioned first in a council etc. Thus, the Second Oecumenical Synod defined by its third canon that the bishop of Constantinople should have "the primacy of honor after the bishop of Rome, for Constantinople is New Rome." The Church recognizes only a primacy of honor and seniority and not of authority over the rest of the bishops in the Church; and in this way and with this spirit she proceeded during the first eight centuries.

The Pope's primacy for the orthodox is a sorrowfull ecclesiastical deviation from the primacy of honor allways granted by the Church to the Pope, a primacy of honor and love, to a primacy of authority.

In the opinion of the Roman Catholic Church, this primacy is not just a title of honor or a presidential primacy but of autonomous authority. The pope was self-proclaimed the vicar of Christ on earth; therefore, he must truly be an authority, a sovereign, and he must have the supreme power over the Christian world.

The criticism of the Orthodox Church of the Pope's primacy is based on the fact that conciliar governance is thus abolished. The synodal system and the Pope's primacy, as developed in the West, are two quite irreconcilable positions in all respects.

Roman catholicism claims that the clergy is above the political power. Consequently, the pope, as head of the clergy, is also the head of the entire world. Pope Nicholas I, who "made himself emperor of the whole world", introduced these

God and man. The distinction made by the fathers between the essence and energies of God supports both the inaccessibility and non-communicability of the divine essence, as well as the communicable nature of God through the divine energies, in other words the possibility granted to each reborn and striving Christian to become a communicant of God.

imperialistic ideas. When the occasion presented itself, he interfered in the affairs of the East without having any right whatsoever; he unfrocked patriarch Photius at a council held in Rome in 863 and, in general, he showed his desire to supervise the affairs of the Eastern Church. Photius responded by unfrocking Nicholas in the council held in 867, because he saw that Nicholas' transgression would have such consequences as to destroy true Church life.

This conflict between Pope Nicholas I and Patriarch Photius was the harbinger of the split of the Eastern and Western Churches.

Thus the unity of the Church received the first blow from the innovations and the monarchical aspirations of the Pope. The Pope, ignoring the fact that the head of the Church is only He who sacrificed Himself for her, the Lord Jesus Christ, whom the Father made *"the head over all things to the church, which is his body"* (Eph. I. 22-23), wanted to become the visible head of the Church and to have supreme authority; he even claimed to be "the successor of the apostle Peter, the most eminent among the apostles" and "vicar of Jesus Christ on Earth." This teaching, however, is absolutely contrary to the spirit of the Bible and of the Fathers of the Church, and its only foundation is the egotistical and absolutist aspiration of the Pope to become leader and despot, judge and sovereign of the whole world.

In 1870, ideed, at the First Vatican Council, the Pope's primacy of authority was established as a dogma.

What a contradiction, indeed, between him and the founder of his religion, of whom he is supposed to be the vicar on earth, who declared that *"my kingdom is not of this world"* (John 18. 36), and, *"whosoever will be great among you, let him be your minister"* (Matth. 20. 26). This opposition of the Pope to the letter and spirit of the Holy Scriptures indicates his departure from the truth, as expressed by the Church, and this departure, of course, places him outside her.

If we study the early Fathers and the Oecumenical Councils of the Church from the first nine centuries, we are fully persuaded that the bishop of Rome was never considered as the supreme authority and infallible head of the Church. Indeed, every bishop is head and president of his own local Church, subject only to the synodical ordinances and decisions of the Church universal, as being alone infallible. Our Lord Jesus Christ alone is the Eternal Prince and Immortal Head of the Church, for *"He is the Head of the body, the church"* (Col. 1. 18)

"Whosoever will be great among you, let him be your minister"
(mosaic icon from the monastery of Osios Lukas)

who said also to His divine disciples and apostles at His ascension into heaven, *"Lo, I am with you always, even unto the end of he world"* (Matth. 28. 20).

In the Holy Scripture, the apostle Peter, whom the papists, relying on the pseudo – Clementines, apocryphal books of he second century, claim to be the founder of the Roman Church and their first bishop, discusses matters as an equal among equals in the apostolic synod of Jerusalem, and at another time is even sharply rebuked by the apostle Paul, as is evident from the Epistle to the Galatians.

Moreover, the papists themselves know well that the very passage of the Gospel on which they base their claims, *"Thou art Peter, and upon this rock I will build my Church"* (Matth. 16. 18), is in the first centuries of the Church interpreted quite differently by all the divine and sacred Fathers without exception. This rock upon which the Lord has built His own church, against which the gates of hell shall not prevail, is understood metaphorically as being Peter's true confession concerning the Lord that He is *"Christ, the Son of the living God"* (Matth. 16. 16). Upon this confession and faith, the saving preaching of the Gospel by all the apostles and their successors rests unshaken. Whence also he apostle Paul, who had been caught up into heaven, evidently interpreting this divine passage, declares by divine inspiration: *"According to the grace of God which is given unto me, as a wise masterbuilder, I have laid the foundation, and another buildeth there on... For other foundation can no man lay than that is laid, which is Jesus Christ"* (I Cor. 3. 10-11).

Imagine how St. Peter himself would react if he had observed these ruses of the papacy to consolidate unscriptural and un-Christian institution, totally in opposition to what Peter had been taught over three successive years by the Lord!

Whoever is of good will and unbiased should read the New Testament, especially the Acts of the Apostles and the passages concerning the council of the Apostles and, then, come to one's conclusions.

St. John the Evangelist was the beloved disciple of Christ, while St. Peter denied Christ thrice. In the synod of the apostles, however, St Peter seems to be first among them

The gathering of the holy Apostles (portable icon of the 17th century)

because he excelled in humility. He never sought any kind of primacy. He always remained a servant, following the example of his Lord.

The sacred Fathers, who held firmly to the apostolic traditions, could not have conceived any idea of an absolute primacy of the apostle Peter and of the bishops of Rome; nor could they have given any interpretation, unknown to the Church, to that passage of the Gospel, but that which was true and right; nor could they arbitrarily have invented by themselves a novel doctrine respecting excessive privileges of the bishop of Rome as successor of Peter; especially since the Church of Rome was chiefly founded not by Peter, whose apostolic ministry in Rome is unrecorded, but by the inspired apostle Paul, whose apostolic ministry in Rome is well known to all.

The divine Fathers, respecting the bishop of Rome only as the bishop of the capital city of the Empire, gave him the honorary prerogative of presidency, and considered him simply as the bishop first in order, that is, first among equals; which prerogative they also assigned afterwards to the bishop of Constantinople, when that city became the capital of the Roman Empire, as the twenty-eighth canon of the fourth Oecumenical Council of Chalcedon bears witness saying, among other things: "We do also determine and decree the same things respecting the prerogatives of the most holy Church of Constantinople, which is New Rome. For the Fathers have rightly given the prerogative to the throne of the elder Rome, because that was the imperial city. And the hundred and fifty most religious bishops, moved by the same consideration, assigned an equal prerogative to the most holy throne of New Rome." From this canon it is very evident that the bishop of Rome is equal in honor to the bishop of the

Church of Constantinople and to those of other Churches, and there is no hint given in any canon or by any of the Fathers that the bishop of Rome has ever been prince of the universal Church, infallible judge of the bishops of the other independent and self-governing Churches, successor to the apostle Peter, or vicar of Jesus Christ on earth.

"Each particular, self-governing Church, both in the East and West, was totally independent and self-administered in the time of the seven Oecumenical Councils. And just as the bishops of the self-governing Churches of the East, so also those of Africa, Spain, Gaul, Germany and Britain managed the affairs of their own Churches, each by their local synods, with the bishop of Rome having no right to interfere. He himself was equally subject and obedient to the decrees of synods. But on important questions which needed the sanction of the universal Church, an appeal was made to an Oecumenical Council, which alone was and is the supreme tribunal in the universal Church.

"Such was the ancient constitution of the Church. None of the bishops ever laid claim to monarchical rights over the universal Church; and if sometimes certain ambitious bishops of Rome raised excessive claims to an absolutism, unknown to the Church, such were duly reproved and rebuked. The assertion, therefore, of the papists that before the period of the great Photius the name of the Roman Throne was holy among all the peoples of the christian world, and that the East, like the West, with one accord and without opposition was subject to the Roman pontiff as lawful successor of the apostle Peter, and consequently vicar of Jesus Christ on earth, is proved to be inaccurate and a manifest error...

"During the nine centuries of the Oecumenical Councils the Eastern Orthodox Church never recognized the excessive claims of primacy on the part of the bishops of Rome, nor consequently did she ever submit herself to them, as Church history plainly bears witness...

"The celebrated Photius, the sacred Prelate and luminary of Constantinople, defending this independence of the Church of Constantinople after the middle of the ninth century, and foreseing the impending perversion of the ecclesiastical constitution in the West and its defection from the orthodox East, at first endeavoured in a peaceful manner to avert the danger; but the bishop of Rome, Nicholas I, by his uncanonical interference with the East, beyond the bounds of his diocese, and by his attempt to subdue the Church of Constantinople to himself, forced matters to the verge of the grievous separation of the Churches."[9]

The God-bearing Fathers, being convinced that History is directed by God and that the Church is governed by Christ, never sought political powers. Desiring to preserve the treasury of faith, they underwent persecutions, exile, and even martyrdom. They never set temporary glory and the powers of this world above their faith. The Papacy, on the contrary, pursuing worldly glory and power, indentified itself with the rulers of this world and consequently it became indifferent to the doctrines of the Church and to the truth of the New Testament, it fell away from the Church, and fell short of the Grace of God.

Saint Mark of Ephesus has declared that, "we consider the Pope as one of the Patriarchs, if he be orthodox."

It is worth noting that even important theologians of the West, for example Hans Küng, refute the primacy and

9. The Reply of the Orthodox Church to Roman Catholic Overtures on Reunion, N. York 1958, p. 18-20.

infallibility of the Pope (newspaper "Boston Sunday Globe", November 16th, 1980).

If it is true that the Lord Jesus Christ placed the apostle Peter above all the other holy apostles, why was the First Apostolic Synod in Jerusalem presided over by the apostle James and not by Peter? And why, eventually, did the opinion of the apostle Paul prevail, being adopted even by the apostle Peter himself?

It is known, as described in the Holy Scriptures, that the apostle Peter stayed for a long time in Antioch and preached to the christians there. Why, then, did he not give such a privilege to the bishops of Antioch? Is it not clear by this event that the claim of the Pope to be successor of the apostle Peter is not based upon Holy Scripture but it is only an invention of the Pope in order to support his monarchical aspirations, which are so contrary not only to the spirit but also to the letter of the Bible?

None of th holy apostles claimed a primary and distinguished position over the other apostles, thus undervaluing and considering them as subordinate. It is because they preserved the spirit of Christ, Who taught humility and simplicity.

The Pope, on the contrary, abandoning the spirit of Christ and losing His Grace, claimed the primacy, forgetting the words of Christ to the apostles John and James, when they asked Him for the first place: *"Ye know not what ye ask"* (Mark. 10. 38).

—·❧ ❁ ❧·—

Later developments in the papal Church come as no surprise. The pope, being the sovereign and ruler of the world, must have his own seat of government in order to house his authority.

It was in this spirit that the papal State was initially established in 755 by Pepin the Short, father of Charlemagne, in exchange for the assistance offered to him by the Pope in becoming the king of Franks. In 1929, the Vatican was acknowledged to be a separate State (a region with a diameter of approximately five kilometers) together with the Lateran (a region with a diameter of one kilometer) by the government of Mussolini.

Pope Pius XI justified this act, since he was both ruler of the Church and of the secular world, with the excuse that "the representative of God on earth cannot possibly be a citizen of an earthly state".

We should stress here how dreadfull this thinking is if we consider that Christ Himself was the citizen of a state. He even accepted to be enrolled in the census in order to abide by the laws of the state, while the pope, the "representative" of Christ on earth cannot possibly be the citizen of an earthly state. The absurdity is manifest. All the holy fathers were citizens of a state located on earth. The kingdom of God is "in heaven", it is spiritual, it does not have any relation with secular power. We could also say that secular power is a deviation from Christianity, since Christ always preached that *"if any man desire to be first, the same shall be last of all, and servant of all"* (St. Mark 9, 35).

Having established his primacy and his infallibility, the pope subsequently claims that "the authority of Church is established insofar as it is established on and is in conformity with the will of the Pope. Without the foregoing, it ceases to exist". For Roman Catholicism, ecumenical councils are nothing more than congresses convened "under the authority, power and chairmanship of the Pope". The bishop Marais must have been right when he wrote: "Roman Catholics would be more accurate if, when reciting the Creed, said "and in one Pope" instead of saying "and in one... Church"*.

2. THE FILIOQUE

The unity of the Church received its first blow when the Pope claimed to be the supreme judge and sovereign, and vicar of Christ on earth. But when one departs from the truth, makes innovations, and serves his egotism and passions, he is deprived of he Grace of God and falls into more errors. So, although during the first eight centuries the Church in the East and West had a unity of faith, the West began to introduce innovations and new doctrines and to adulterate the true faith. Its first error and heresy, and departure from the doctrines of the Fathers and of the Oecumenical Councils, was the addition of the "Filioque" to the Creed.

Filioque refers to the Western dogma of the procession of the Holy Spirit, concerning Its nature and not Its operations. The main biblical source on which the Fathers of the Church relied for establishing the Orthodox dogma was the Gospel of St. John (chapter 15: 26): *"But when the Comforter comes, whom I will send unto you from the Father, even the Spirit of truth, which proceedeth from the Father, He shall testify of Me"*.

In these words of Christ Himself, the Holy Spirit proceeds from the Father and is sent into the world by the Son. «Therefore, there are two functions: "procession" and "mission". In the procession, the "source" is the Father; in the mission it is the Son. The procession happens outside of time, the mission happens within time. Procession concerns the Holy

---

*We should point out here that the desire of the Pope to be sovereign is proven by the three crowns the tiara of the Popes bears, these symbolizing his authority over: a) earth, b) hell and c) heaven.

Trinity, mission concerns the world. This is abundantly clear
from the words of the Lord quoted above... Either the Western
Church confuses the 'procession' with the 'mission' or is
deliberately closing its eyes to what is self-evident»
(Archimandrite V. Bakoyannis, ONE LORD, ONE FAITH,
pp. 44-45).

"During the Second Oecumenical Council this very
question was settled once and for all by the use in the Creed of
the word "procession" to describe the manner of existence of
the Holy Spirit, which constitutes His special individuality.
Thus the Father is unbegotten, i.e. derives His existence from
no-one; the Son is from the Father by generation. The Holy
Spirit is from the Father not by generation, but by procession.
The Father is cause, the Son and the Spirit are caused. The
difference between the Son and the Spirit is that One is caused
by generation and the Other by procession...

"The whole doctrine of the Trinity may be broken down into
two simple statements:
  a) What is common in the Holy Trinity is common to and
     identical in all three Persons or Hypostases.
  b) What is of the Hypostasis or of the Person, i.e. a
     hypostatic property, or manner of existence, is
     individual and belongs only to one Person or Hypostasis
     of he Holy Trinity."[10]
The Latins claim that the Holy Spirit proceeds "from the
Father and the Son" because, according to St. Augustine's
teaching, "whatever the Father has, the Son also has."

But in answer to this argument St. Photius said: "If all things
common to the Father and the Son are necessarily common to
the Spirit... and if the procession is common to the Father and
the Son, the Spirit therefore will then proceed from Himself;

---

10. J. Romanides, "The Filioque", pp. 13, 24.

and He will be principle of Himself, and both cause and caused; a thing which even the myths of the ancient Greeks never fabricated."[11]

Following the teaching of St Augustine, the Frankish theological tradition inserted the Filioque into the Creed, though the Eighth Oecumenical Council of 879 condemned those who either add to or subtract from the Nicene-Constantinopolitan Creed and those who did not accept the Seventh Oecumenical Council, even if did not mention the Franks by name.

There is also a letter of Pope John to St. Photius in which the Filioque is described as something newly added but never used in the Church of Rome, and that it is vigorously condemned.

The same Pope John accepted the Eighth Oecumenical Council's condemnation of the Filioque, not only as being an addition to the Creed but also as a teaching.

According to the seventh canon of the Council of Ephesus and the exposition of faith drawn up at the First Oecumenical Council, the Church strictly prohibits the use of any other creeds except the Nicene-Constantinopolitan one, with the penalty, in case of disobedience, that bishops be deposed and that the laity be excommunicated.

The Fathers of the Fourth Oecumenical Council of Chalcedon, on reading the Creed, said: "This Holy Creed is sufficient for the full knowledge of the truth, for it contains in itself the full doctrine on the Father, the Son, and the Holy Spirit."

Even St Cyril (†444), whose teachings were misunderstood by the Latins who used them in order to justify the addition of the Filioque to the Creed, writes: "We prohibit any change

---

11. Ibid, p. 25.

whatever in the Creed of Faith drawn up by the Holy Nicene
Fathers. We do not allow ourselves or anyone else to change or
omit one word or syllable in that Creed."

The same St Cyril elsewhere emphasizes: "The holy
Oecumenical Council assembled at Ephesus has prohibited the
introduction into God's Church of any confession of faith,
except the one existing, which was handed down to us by the
blessed Fathers, through whom the Holy Spirit did speak."[12]

The theologians of the West have misinterpreted the
teaching of St Cyril in the words, "though the Spirit proceeds
from the Father, still He is not alien to the Son, for the Son has
everything jointly with the Father."[13]

The true meaning of St Cyril's words, however, is that the
Holy Spirit is consubstantial with the Son, as the same St Cyril
writes elsewhere: "...the Spirit of God the Father, which
proceedeth from Him, but is not alien to the Son, as regards
His essence."[14] And again, "...the Holy Spirit not receiving His
existence from or through the Son, but as proceeding from the
Father and proper to the Son."[15]

Pope Agatho also wrote to the Greek Emperor: "...the
Church of Rome upholds the faith delivered by the five
Oecumenical Councils, and takes great care that all things
defined by the canons should remain unchanged, nothing
added or taken away, and be kept inviolate both in words and
thoughts."[16]

We must bring to mind here that all present at the Second
Oecumenical Council of Nicea, after listening to this Creed,

---

12. The History of the Council of Florence, Boston 1971, p.79
13. Ibid, p. 113
14. Ibid, p. 114
15. Ibid, p. 114
16. Ibid, p. 69-70

exclaimed: "We all believe this; we all think alike. This is the faith of the Apostles, this is the Orthodox faith... Let him who receives not this faith be excommunicated."

Even in the very Church of Rome the Creed was read without the addition for a long time after the Seventh Oecumenical Council. In this form (without the addition) it was engraved by order of Pope Leo III (795-816), on silver

The Seventh Oecumenical Council (Monastery of Metamorphosis, Meteora)

tablets, in Greek and Latin, and placed in front of the church of St. Peter in Rome.

We must also note that the oldest Latin copies of the acts of the Oecumenical Councils do not contain the addition to the Creed.

The Fathers of the succeeding Oecumenical Councils had received and confirmed the Creed in the same form, in which it was left to the Church by the two first Oecumenical Councils; they did not make any change in it. They forbade any addition to the Creed, even in case of necessity.

The Fathers of the Church avoided adding even the word "Theotokos" to the Creed, though the notion expressed by this word is nothing more than a short explanation of the doctrine contained in the Creed, and the addition itself was useful and necessary as a refutation of the Nestorians.

Any such additions to the Creed, even if they were really explanations, were strictly forbidden after the Council of Ephesus.

Thus the eastern fathers, obeying the decrees of the Councils, and mindful of their oath, could not admit the addition of the Filioque to the Creed to be a right and lawful one. How could an individual Church arrogate to herself the right of adding to the Creed when this right was prohibited by the Councils even to the Church Catholic?

The Fathers of the Church and the confessors of faith were ready, for Christ's and His Gospel's sake, to lay down their souls, bodies, blood, and all that they had on earth for "in things of faith there must be no concessions, no waverings."

It is noteworthy that even the Emperor of Byzantium, when at Florence for the union of the Churches and despite his desire for it, said then that, "the Latins dispute what is self-evident, and induce the Greeks to agree to what has been amathematised by the Oecumenical Councils. Does not this evince an endeavour to make the one, holy, Catholic Church condradict herself?"[17]

It is important to realize that all doctrines were promulgated in the Greek language and then translated into Latin. So it is very reasonable to suppose that the Greeks should understand Greek better than foreigners.

St. Basil the Great says that, "the Holy Spirit proceeds only

---

17. Ibid, p. 186

from the Father, and not from anyone else."[18] If the spirit proceeds from the Person of the Father, then the expression *"not from anyone else"* shows that he does not proceed from another Person.

St Gregory the Theologian says that, "everything the Father has belongs to the Son, with the exception of causality."[19]

The term *"Procession"* in the Creed was introduced as a parallel to *"Generation"* and both meant *causal relation* to the Father and not energy or mission.

St Maximus The Confessor († 662) also assures Marinus, to whom he is writing, that "the Romans of the West accept that the Holy Spirit proceeds causally only from the Father, and that the Son is not cause."[20]

We must not forget that when the Latins insisted that the Filioque was an improvement of an already good, but not complete doctrine concerning the Holy Spirit, Pope Leo warned that "when one attempts to improve what is good, he should first be sure that in trying to improve he is not really corrupting."[21] He emphasized that he could not put himself above the Fathers of the Councils who omitted the Filioque neither by oversight nor out of ignorance, but by divine inspiration. This theological position is the same with that of Pope Hadrian I (772-795) and also with that of the Toledo Councils where the Filioque is not in the Creed.

In 1009, however, the frankish pope Sergius IV, during his enthronement address, added the Filioque to the Creed; a little later Pope Benedict VIII introduced the Creed including the Filioque into the worship of the Church. The heresy was now

---

18. Ibid, p. 97
19. Ibid, p. 112
20. J. Romanides, The Filioque, p.9
21. Ibid, p.12

an established fact and the pope was erased from the diptychs of the Orthodox Church.

The insistence of later Popes upon their heretical teaching of the Filioque and of the Primacy of Pope, which is no more than a misunderstanding of the primacy of honour that was granted to him by the other equal Patriarchates, caused the schism between the two Churches. Every good-willed investigator will clearly see that the Eastrern Church only desired to remain in the faith of the Fathers and to preserve the unity of faith, i.e. to remain in the Orthodox Church – the Truth – because outside of her there is no salvation.

We ask the Western Church: "Have not the holy fathers of both East and West in joint aggreement at the Council of Nicaea defined this dogma? How can one party decide unilaterly to change this dogma, without even taking into account the opinion of the other party? Does the Holy Bible state anywhere that the Holy Spirit proceeds also from the Son? Nowhere. On the contrary, it is explicitly and clearly stated that the Holy Spirit proceeds from the Father. So, what were your grounds for such an addition?"

This crucial question demonstrates the persistence of the Eastern Church in the conciliar system and the inclination of the Western Church to arbitrariness and authoritarianism, which later led the same Church to further ecclesiastical and dogmatic deviations. This is why many people claim that Roman-Catholicism is the first protestant Church.

St. Symeon of Thessaloniki writes that if the Holy Spirit proceeded from the Son as well, the Son Himself would have revealed that to us, in the same way He revealed to us that the Holy Spirit is sent by Him. Adding the Filioque is as if we attribute to the Son a quality He does not reveal anywhere. Who knows better about the eternal procession of the Holy

Spirit: we or Christ?

The orthodox always remained faithful to tradition, to the faith handed down to them from the first apostolic Church. The papists, on the contrary, from the time they cut themselves off from the body of the Church, fell into more and more dogmatic errors, thus widening the gap that had opened between the Churches.

III. What other differences exist between the churches that keep us separate even now?

1. INFALLIBILITY

As we have said, the Eastern and Apostolic Church believes that the Truth is identified with Christ *("I am the way, the truth and the life")* and is expressed in His Church, which is His body. The apostle Paul says clearly that the Church is *"the pilllar and the ground of the truth"* (I Tim. 3.15). The truth that Christ delivered to us is preserved in and expressed by the Church of Christ. The Russian theologian Bulgakov says that "infallibility belongs to the Church." The fathers of the Church never trusted in themselves or in any single person as an authority, for occasionally even the greatest Fathers erred in some matter or diverged somewhat from the consensus of the faithful. Rather they trusted only in the Church, as expressed by the Oecumenical Councils.

Even the promise of Christ, *"where two or three are gathered together in my name, there am I in the midst of them"* (Matth. 18.20), proves that Christ is present not where one person decides, but where two or more consult and ask for the enlightment of God. Nowhere in the New Testament is it mentioned that Christ gave to any person special privileges and rights, not even to the apostle Peter, whose exclusive successor is supposed to be the Pope, but, on the contrary, the synodical system is manifest everywhere.

The Roman Church, however, in the nineteenth century she proclaimed, to the astonishment of the Christian World, that the bishop of Rome is infallible.

The First Vatican Council in 1870 proclaimed that whenever the pope speaks ex cathedra on matters of faith, he is considered infallible. Even if the pope concerned is proven corrupted, his decision is deemed infallible and whoever disagrees with the pope is to be excommunicated.

The infallibility of the pope suffices to overturn completely Christian ecclesiology. From the moment that a council decided that only the pope is infallible, this council has betrayed the faith and belief shared by all Christians that only the Church is infallible, functioning properly in councils, but never a single bishop, no matter what he ranks. However, we now have before us a tremendous and scandalous dilemma.

The council resolved that only the pope is infallible. Therefore, a council could make mistakes. Thus, if a council accepts that it could make mistakes, how could it possibly resolve that the pope is infallible? Might it not be argued that the resolution of the council is erroneous?

Such ridiculous conclusions multiply when egotism and vanity prevail and oppress even common sense.

The teachings on the infallibility of the pope distort the Church and do away with its synodal operation.

The Orthodox Eastern Church of Christ knows of no one infallible upon earth, with the exception of the Son and Word of God, who was ineffably made man. Even the apostle Peter himself thrice denied the Lord and the apostle Paul twice rebuked him for not walking uprightly according to the truth of the Gospel.

When the question arose whether the christians should keep the decrees of the Mosaic Law, what did the apostles do? As is mentioned in the Acts: *"And the apostles and the elders came together to consider of this matter"* (Acts 15.6). They did not consult the apostle Peter as the only bearer of the truth and vicar of Christ on earth, what the Pope wants him to be, but they convoked a synod where, together with the apostles, even the elders (presbyters) were present. This behaviour of the apostles is noteworthy because they had themselves known the Lord, had learned from Him the saving truth of the Gospel, and had been imbued with divine inspiration, when baptized in the Holy Spirit on the day of Pentecost.

Is this not a proof that the truth is declared only by the Church and that only the Church must decide in questions concerning the salvation of her members?

And is it not blasphemy to set the Pope over the Synods when even the apostles themselves never claimed such a privilege?

All human beings are imperfect and may commit errors at any time. No one is infallible. Judas spent three years of his life as a disciple of Christ, he even wrought miracles. None the less, this did not prevent him from falling.

In essence, the principle of infallibility is an attempt of the pope to identify himself personally with self-truth, Christ Himself. These are the foolish consequences of an unrestrained desire for supremacy and power! By declaring his own

The Pentecost

infallibility, the pope seems to declare: "I am the truth!" Wherein, then, does he fall short of declaring himself Christ?

Observe carefully the way the apostles expressed the results of their disputes during that Apostolic Synod: *"For it seemed good to the Holy Ghost, and to us"* (Acts 15.28), i.e. during their consultations the Holy Spirit was present and directed the thoughts of the members of the synod who sat and conversed as equals. None of them claimed infallibility or primacy, which the Pope so insistently demands, thus proving how much he has strayed from the spirit and tradition of the apostles.

The infallibility of the Pope is denied not only by the orthodox but even by important papal theologians, e.g. Hans Küng, who refuses to accept both primacy and infallibility (newspaper "Boston Sunday Globe," November 16th, 1980), August Bernard Hasler etc. Even the Synod of Constantia declared that the Pope is not infallible and emphasized that he (the Pope) is just one of the bishops.

Moreover, how can we accept the doctrine of infallibility or primacy from history, when so many Popes have been anathematized or deposed by councils of bishops? It is well-known that Pope Liberius, in the fourth century, subscribed an Arian confession; likewise Zosimus, in the fifth century, approved a heretical confession denying original sin. Virgilius, in the sixth century, was condemned for wrong opinions by the fifth Council; The same (Virgilius) had accepted the Council's right to condemn him. Honorius, having fallenn into the monothelite heresy, was condemned in the seventh century by the Sixth Oecumenical Council as a heretic and the Popes who succeeded him (Leo and Andrian) acknowledged and accepted his condemnation.

Such facts caused the peoples of the West to protest against innovations and to demand a return to the ecclesiastical constitution of the first centuries. The same was done in the seventeenth century by the learned Gallican theologians, and in the 19th century, in the years 1870, the christian consciousness protested, in the persons of the celebrated clerics and theologians of Germany, because of the novel dogma of papal infallibility proclaimed by the Vatican Council. A consequence of this protest was the formation of the separate religious communities of the Old Catholics, who have disowned the papacy and are independent of it.

The Russian theologian Bulgakov has declared that, "the Roman-catholic bishops by their decision concerning infallibility, have dogmatized and signed an act that is equal to canonical suicide."[22]

Indeed, by this novel dogma, unprecedented in ecclesiastical history, the Roman-catholic church abolishes the authority of the Oecumenical Councils, because their power and infallibility were surrendered to the bishop of Rome, who, on this account, is no more a bishop in the Church. He has become some fantastic and inconceivable being who stands above the bishops and above the Church which could not exist without him. In other words, the Church has been replaced by the Pope of Rome.

Such errors and motivations indicate to any good-willed Christian that any doctrine springing therefrom must evidently be false.

2. THE IMMACULATE CONCEPTION

Roman-catholicism, having departed from truth continued to formulate new doctrines, contrary to the spirit and tradition

---

22. Bulgacov, *L' Orthodoxie*, p.82

of the Gospels and in accord with its spirit of rationalism, and in the 19th century, the dogma of the immaculate conception of the Most Holy Virgin was proclaimed.

"The one, holy, catholic, and apostolic Church of the Seven Oecumenical Councils teaches that, the supernatural incarnation of the only-begotten Son and Word of God, of the Holy Spirit and the Virgin Mary, is alone pure and immaculate;

The Most Holy Virgin (portable icon from the monastery of Osios Lukas)

but the papal Church again made an innovation by laying down a novel dogma concerning the immaculate conception of the Mother of God and ever-Virgin Mary, which was unknown to the ancient Church and strongly opposed at different times even by the more distinguished among the papal theologians."[23]

Can we possibly believe that the Church was in error for nineteen centuries and that only now the truth has been revealed by the Pope? Nowhere in the Gospels, in the decrees of the Councils or in the works of the Fathers is there found this teaching of the Roman-catholics.

3. PURGATORY

Another novel and un-orthodox teaching of the Roman-catholics is the superabundance of the merits of the saints. They teach that the good works or merits of the most Holy Virgin and of the saints are more than they need to save themselves and, therefore, the rest of them can be used for the forgiveness of the sins of other men. Of course, the dispensation of these merits has been assumed by the Pope himself, who invented many ways to gather money through the administration of this supposed right to forgive sins.

As Professor P. Trembelas sets forth in his treatise on dogmatics (volume C, Athens 1961, p. 284), the pope allocated his power to the remaining clergy on a proportionate basis: "The Pope has absolute authority over absolution through the issuing of indulgences. Each bishop in his diocese is entitled to provide release or indulgences of fifty days from temporal penalties for sin, while metropolitans and cardinals may grant absolution of one hundred and two hundred days respectively.

The Bible, however, is clear in this matter and warns us that

23. J. Romanides, The Filioque, p.15

every man will be judged *"according to that he hath done, whether it be good or bad"* (II Cor. 5.10). Each man's sins can be cleansed only by sincere repentance and by his conformation to the divine commandments, and not by the surplus merits of the saints' good works.

An equally un-orthodox and un-scriptural dogma is that of the purgatorial fire wherein the sinful souls stay for a shorter or longer period, in proportion to the number and weight of their sins, in order to be cleansed and purified from guilt.

The Lord, however, spoke about an eternal hell only, which the sinful and the unrepentant will suffer, and about an eternal life which the righteous and the repentant will enjoy. Nowhere did he speak about a middle condition where a soul must be purified in order to be saved. The Church believes the words of the Gospel, that both the righteous and the sinful await the resurrection of the dead, and that they enjoy in advance Paradise or Hell, in proportion to their good or bad works, before their final placement. The apostle Paul says: *"And these all, having obtained a good report through faith, received not the promise; God having provided some better thing for us, that they without us should not be made perfect"* (Hebr. 11.39-40).

4. THE DIVINE EUCHARIST

For more than a thousand years throughout East and West the one, united, catholic, and apostolic Church, according to the example of our Saviour, used leavened bread in the divine Eucharist, a fact acknowledged by all truth-loving papal theologians. Since the eleventh century, however, the papal Church made an innovation in the sacrament of the divine Eucharist by introducing unleavened bread, contrary to the ancient tradition of the Church universal. Another innovation of the papal Church is that it claims to consecrate the precious gifts (the bread and wine) only by the utterance of the Lord's words: *"Take, eat; this is my body"* and *"Drink ye all of it; for this is my blood"* (Matth. 26: 26.28), while in the early Church, as the ancient rituals of Rome and Gaul testify, the precious gifts were consecrated by the invocation of the Holy Spirit; the Holy Spirit consecrates the gifts and not the priest himself.

"Drink ye all of it; for this is my blood"
(fresco from the monastery of Varlaam, Meteora)

The papal Chuch has also deprived the laity of the Holy Chalice, though our Lord commanded *"Drink ye all of it"*, and the early Church universally obeyed His command. It is worth noting that many ancient orthodox bishops of Rome had prohibited the use of wafers in the Divine Eucharist, but later Popes abolished the giving of the holy chalice to the laity and imposed the use of wafers.

5. THE BAPTISM

One more innovation of the Roman-catholics is that they abandoned the ancient order of baptism with three immersions. The word "baptism" comes from the Greek word «βαπτίζω» that means "to immerse". The ancient, united Church used to baptize by three immersions in the water. Pope Pelagius II (6th cent.) speaks of the triple immersion as a command of the Lord. This also agrees with what the apostle Paul says: *"Know ye not, that so many of us as were baptized into Jesus Christ were baptized into His death? Therefore we are buried with him by baptism into death; that like as Christ was raised up from the dead by the glory of the Father, even so we also should walk in newness of life"* (Rom. 6. 3-4). The three immersions symbolize the three day burial of Christ, our Saviour, and His Resurrection. The same way Christ was buried in His tomb, so are we buried in the water and resurrected as a new man from sin.

The sacred fonts that still exist in very ancient churches of Italy, where baptism by immersion prevailed until the thirteenth century, are the most eloquent witnesses of the truth. Nevertheless, the Popes, continuing their descent into innovation, accepted baptism by sprinkling or affusion, showing how much have compomised to the spirit of the world.

IV. The Protestants

As stated above, the Western Church took advantage of its un-ecclesiastical teaching on purgatorial fire and the superabundance of the merits of the saints to proceed to actions that scandalized the faithful.

Putting forward the excuse that they needed to raise funds for constructing St. Peter's basilica in Rome, the Western Church issued the so-called indulgences. Pursuant according to the Pope's teachings, anyone who bought these indulgences could buy off the sins of his dead relatives, thus conveying them from the sufferings of purgatory to paradise. So, a host of believers hastened to obtain these "magic" papers that would lead them straight to paradise, even if those particular persons for whom the purchase was made, had died without repenting. Therefore, they were led to the clear but erroneous conclusion that they could lead a careless life on earth and buy paradise as well. Of course, this view distorts the Holy Scriptures and the teaching of the Church.

This action of the papal Church was plainly simony, since its purpose was to gather money, even if the true teaching of the Church was perverted. Seeing this arbitrary behavior and the un-Christian teachings and acts of the papal Church, many pious and sensitive clergymen were alarmed and resisted. Among those clergymen Luther, Calvin and Zwingli distinguished themselves. Followed by many disciples, these three faithful Catholic men assailed vehemently the arbitrary and un-ecclesiastical behavior of their Church. Of course, none of them was heard.

Thus, when once in Toledo a part of the Western Church decided to change the Creed of Nicaea and gave rise to the first schism between the two Churches, now almost one thousand years later another part of the Western Church dissented with tits leadership. They strongly opposed to the arbitrary acts of the papal Church and were split from it. They had two options: either to return to the One Church or to follow their own way. Unfortunately, they opted for the second. In this way the Protestant Church was founded. This Church later split into hundreds of denominations, each one of them claiming for itself the truth. They made exactly the same mistake with the Church from which they had split. They decided to interpret truth in their own way, without referring to the ancient and united ecumenical Church.

-ε-ξ3-ξ3-ξ3-3-

Protestants deny tradition, i.e. the interpretation assigned to the holy texts by the apostles and their immediate successors.

Yet it is protestants themselves who interpret the texts according to their own viewpoint and, thus, are led to errors. The fact that they have split into hundreds of denominations and factions, each one of them claiming infallibility and truth for itself, is the greatest proof of their error. Christ is the incarnation of the truth. He said it Himself: *"I am the way, and the truth and the life"* (St. John 14, 6). And as St. Paul confesses, *"Christ is not divided"* (see I Cor. 1, 13). Christ cannot be divided, cannot be split. A truth that is not the whole truth is no longer true, but a lie. The Branch Theory, that each Church or Denomination supposedly holds part of the truth, and that altogether they hold the entire truth, is completely untenable, even when judged by common sense.

Protestants declare that the only inspired text they accept is the Scriptures (Sola Scriptura). The Holy Scriptures, however, do not indicate anywhere that they are the only books inspired by God and that such inspiration by God is limited thereto. They do not preclude the possibility of other texts inspired by God appearing later on. On what grounds, therefore, do Protestants deny divine inspiration to subsequent authors and, especially, the ecumenical councils convened after the examples of the Council of the Apostles?

We believe in the Scriptures because they were handed down to us by tradition. Whoever denies tradition, by which we believe in the Holy Scriptures, will challenge the authenticity of the Scriptures themselves.

We should also take into account that the Church existed even before the Holy Scriptures. When the apostles dispersed into the world to preach Christ, no written Gospel existed. Nevertheless, the Church existed. It relied on the witness and experience of the apostles, namely on oral tradition.

Reacting to the teaching of the papal Church, that salvation is by works, the protestants professed that salvation is solely by faith and not through works or through struggle for inner perfection. Therefore, monasticism and asceticism were useless to them.

Of the sacraments, Protestants accept only baptism and Holy Communion, because they are based on biblical references. However, they do not believe in the transformation of the bread and wine into the body and blood of Christ. From the Western Church they kept only the filioque and the theory of predestination, but they completely abolished fasting.

Protestants claim that man is saved solely "by faith", although St. James states clearly that *"faith without works is dead" and "what doth it profit... though a man say he hath faith and have not works? Can faith save him?"* (James, 2:26, 14). But, could anyone have right faith without this faith leading him to pious works? Devout faith cannot be dead.

The New Testament sets forth numerous times that Christ gave the apostles (and their successors) the power to *"bind and loose"* the sins of mankind. The Orthodox, as well as the Roman Catholic Church, interpreting correctly these passages, established confession so that the priests (successors of the apostles) could absolve the sins of people or not. *"Whose soever sins ye remit, they are remitted unto them; and whose soever sins ye retain, they are retained"* (John, 20: 23). The priests can only know which sins can be absolved and which not, by learning of them. And the priests can only be aware of such sins, if the believers confess them. There is no other way.

Protestants even abolished this commandment and confess directly to God. They claim that there can be no intermediary between God and a man's heart. Man has direct access to God. Also shame might hinder a true confession. This teaching shows that they do not have humility, and *"a broken and contrite"* heart. A truly humble and contrite man will confess in front of anyone and not just in front of a priest.

Some protestants reject also the sign of the cross because it is supposedly a symbol of disgrace, since Christ was crucified on a cross. But it is exactly because Christ was crucified that the cross was converted from a symbol of disgrace into a symbol of blessing, a symbol of victory. Have they never read what St. Paul wrote to the Galatians? *"But God forbid that I should glory, save in the cross of our Lord Jesus Christ, by whom the world is crucified unto me, and I unto the world"* (Galatians, 6:14). Do they really claim that they are more faithful or pious than St. Paul? And since protestants believe solely in the Holy Scriptures, do they know of any passage preventing us from believing in the power of the cross and making its sign upon our body?

Protestants violate both the divine commandments and the practice of Christ Himself and of the apostles as far as fasting is concerned. Christ fasted without needing to do so, just to set an example for us. He also ordered his disciples to fast. We learn from the New Testament (Acts 14:23; 2 Corinthians, 11:27) that the first Christians fasted following the commandment of Christ and the apostles. Christ himself said: *"The days will come, when the bridegroom shall be taken from them, and then shall they fast"* (Matthew, 9:15). Obeying this order, the Orthodox Church established fasting after Christ ascended into heaven.

Unfortunately, it seems that not only did protestants reject tradition but they also abridged or distorted passages of the Holy Scriptures. This is where their scholastic theology has led them.

Protestants have distanced themselves so far from the

Church and are so dominated by a rationalizing spirit that denies the mystery of God and the Church, that they have reached such extremes as ordaining women or celebrating marriages between homosexuals. They prove that they are a purely humanistic organization which is in no way related to God.

If Catholicism has so many differences with the One Church, protestant denominations have vastly many more. The renowned, non-Orthodox, Byzantine expert Stephen Runciman appears to be right when he stated in 1994 in London: "Roman catholics and protestants rationalize everything with a great ease but they forget that, at bottom, religion is mystical", namely it transcends rationalism.

༘༘༘༘༘

Protestants appeared around A.D. 1500. For 1,500 years they did not exist. However, the Lord said: *"I am with you always"* (Matthew, 28:20). He did not say "I will be with you after 1,500 years" but *"I am with you"* henceforth; without any interruption, to the end of time. Christ does not lie. And, of course, He could not possibly be absent for 1,500 years until protestants discovered Him.

Throughout these 1,500 years, until the Protestants made their appearance, there was a Church led by Christ, as confirmed by Him. Otherwise, protestants themselves would not exist. They claim that the Church had been deceived for 1,500 years and was waiting for them to put everything in order. Now, if we take into account the aforementioned words of the Lord that He is with his disciples (and their successors) for the rest of their lives and He will be to the end of time, protestants are correcting Christ Himself, even though unconsciously.

Should they not ask themselves where was Christ all those years when the Church, in their opinion, was deceived? Did Christ coexist with error and lies or was He totally absent? Behold, to what insane conclusions we are led if we take Protestant assertions at their face value.

V. What are the presuppositions for a true and godly union

The unity of all men under one faith was and is the most fervent petition of the Great Highpriest, our Lord Jesus Christ. He prayed for this unity in His Last Prayer, a short time before His sacrifice on the Cross. It is the duty of every christian to pray and to strive for the unity of all christians; a unity, however, in the body of Christ, in His Church, in His Truth.

«Orthodoxy, which through Christ came into the world and history as a divine and eternal truth, lives perpetually in Christ and always exists in the world, in the body of Christ, in His ONE, HOLY, CATHOLIC AND APOSTOLIC CHURCH.

»Thus, the quest of contemporary christians in their

meetings and dialogues, should be **whether the existing "Churches" and Confessions are united in Orthodoxy (Truth) as it was revealed by Christ, and not whether they are united to one another.** For it is possible to find a unity based on external and conventional bonds and not on revealed truth.

»Scientific and theological investigation of christian sources, if it is carried out with humility and a sincere love for truth and not with an A PRIORI interpretation, will help each one of the so called "Churches" and Confessions discover the Orthodoxy of the ONE Church.

»Such a process of return to Orthodoxy-true belief-has as a presupposition *common repentance,* i.e. one's willingness to admit heresy, if there is such, its rejection, and one's reunion with the One Church of Christ. This One Church, by the Grace of God, was never limited to one region of the earth but was always spread throughout the world. So it is possible for every

"Joy shall be in heaven over one sinner that repententh" (Luk 15,7)

existing "Church" to find her. This can be done only by the return of the existing "Churches" to the Orthodox Church existing in their area whence, at a certain point of their history, they were separated...

»It is, therefore, possible for the christians of the West, who belong to the Roman-catholic "Church" or to whatever other Christian Confession, to recover their old and original form, by their return to ancient, orthodox Rome and to the faith of their orthodox Fathers, who did not accept any of the heretical tenets of today's Rome (Primacy, Infallibility, Filioque etc). When the Roman-catholic Church becomes the true continuation of the Orthodox Church she can help the many divisions of Protestantism return to Orthodoxy which unfortunately was not done by the Reformation of the 16th century.»[24]

A true union, therefore, is possible only in the truth and in the exactness of the doctrines, as they were expressed by the Oecumenical Councils and by the Fathers of the Church. For only this way will it be a saving union in Christ and not according ro human desire.

The Eastern orthodox Church of Christ, "is ready heartily to accept all that which both the Eastern and Western Churches unanimously professed before the ninth century, if she has perchance perverted or does not hold it. And if the Westerners prove from the teaching of the holy Fathers and the divinely assembled Oecumenical Councils that the then orthodox Roman Church, which was throughout the West, even before the ninth century read the Creed with the addition, or used unleavened bread, or accepted the doctrine of a purgatorial fire, or sprinkling instead of baptism, or the immaculate conception of the ever-Virgin, or the temporal power, or the

---

24. G. Metallinos, "What is Orthodoxy?", pp. 27-28

infallibility and the absolutism of the bishop of Rome, we have no more to say. But if, on the contrary, it is plainly demonstrated, as those of the Latins themselves who love the truth, also acknowledge, that the Eastern and Orthodox Catholic Church of Christ holds fast the anciently transmitted doctrines which were at that time professed in common both in the East and the West, and that the Western Church perverted them by divers innovations, then it is clear, even to children, that the more natural way to union is the return of the Western Church to the ancient doctrinal and administrative condition of things; for the faith does not change in any way with time or circumstances, but remains the same alawys and everywhere, for *"there is one body and one Spirit"* it is said, *"even as ye are called in one hope of your calling; one Lord, one faith, one baptism, one God and Father of all, who is above all, and through all, and in you all."* (Eph. 4: 5-6)[25]

In the Fathers of the apostolic Church, we orthodox find the ancient and divinely-transmitted doctrines, which we carefully hold fast up to the present time. Nowhere do we find the innovations which were later brought forth in the West, and which the papal Church adopted and retains till this very day.

The Eastern Orthodox Church deems that only those who live in an ascetic manner, whose soul is imbued with the grace of the Holy Spirit, are able to formulate correctly whatever concerns faith and theology. The Western Church trusts solely those whose mind is filled with secular knowledge. This is the main difference between the two Churches. On the one hand it shows the persistence of the Orthodox in the overshadowing and illumination of the Holy Spirit and, on the other hand, it manifests the faith of the Western people in the strength of the mind and in rationalism. In other words, the difference lies

---

25. The Reply ... pp.10-11

between faith in the supernatural and divine, and in rationalizing everything. On the one part there is a Church looking to revelation, to God, and on the other part there is a Church focused on man, namely a secular organization that is simply called Christian.

It is self-evident to every right-thinking person that without faith in Christ it is impossible to please God; but it is self-evident, too, that this salutary faith in Christ ought by all means to be true in everything, and in agreement with the Holy Scripture and the apostolic traditions, upon which the teaching of the divine Fathers and the holy, divinely-assembled Councils is founded. Moreover, it is manifest that the universal Church of God, which holds fast entire in its bosom this unique, unadulterated, and salutary faith as a divine trust just as it was formulated and delivered during the first nine centuries by the God-bearing Fathers, who were inspired by the Spirit, is one and the same for ever, not manifold and varying with the course of time; the gospel truths are never susceptible to alteration or development in course of time, like the various philosophical systems; for *"Jesus Christ is the same yesterday, and today, and for ever"* (Heb. 13.8).

We should note that even non-Orthodox intellectuals and ecclesiastical personages, like the first Secretary General of the World Council of Churches, VISSER T' HOOFT, Cardinal ETCHEGARY, and the great Byzantine expert, Stephen Runciman, have acknowledged that the Eastern tradition has preserved substantial elements of the Church, the proper teaching on the Holy Spirit, holy communion, councils, etc.

An honest reader can have no doubt which of the communions is the true successor to the Church of the holy Fathers and which of them has been altered by heresies and innovations. He must not doubt at all that if he really wants to follow the truth, he must approach the tradition of Christ, of the apostles, and of the Fathers of the seven Oecumenical Counsils. Within this tradition he can find the true Church of Christ, the truth, and Orthodoxy, outside of which there is no salvation. Any Church which upholds this tradition possesses Orthodoxy. Any Church which has departed from this tradition has departed from the truth i.e. from Christ.

A true union of the Churches, therefore, is possible only with the revival of the ancient symbols (creeds) and tradition, which were followed by the God-bearing Fathers, and with the return to the faith of the first and united Church.

We cannot doubt that since the Pope of Rome claimed to be the sovereign and despot of the world, he lost the Grace of God and fell into many other dogmatic beliefs, contrary to the teaching of the Gospel and of the Fathers of the Church. We do not doubt that the primacy and infallibility of the Pope are based neither upon the teaching of the Holy Scriptures nor upon that of the Fathers of the Church.

Is it possible to believe in the infallibility of the Pope, when so many Popes were condemned by Oecumenical or Local Councils, and other Popes were well-known for their corrupt life? Is it possible to believe that the primacy of honor, given to the Pope by the Church, because Rome was then the capital of the Roman Empire (primus inter pares honoris causa), meant that the Pope would have authority over the Church, when ever since the epoch of the holy apostles the synodical system prevailed in the Church?

There can be no doubt that the Eastern, Orthodox Church of Christ has retained the tradition of her Fathers unadulterated, has kept unchanged the faith she has received, without adding anything or subtracting anything from what the holy apostles have delivered and the holy Fathers have preserved. No sober and good-willed investigator of history can prove the contrary of it. Even the Latins, when they heard the orthodox doctrines expressed by the Greek Fathers in the Council of Florence, said: "we had never heard anything of the sort before; the Greeks teach more correctly than the Latin theologians" (Syropulus vi 19).

St. Peter also states in his second catholic epistle (chapter 3:16) that in the Holy Bible *"are some things hard to be understood, which they that are unlearned and unstable wrest, as they do also the other scriptures, unto their own destruction"*. The distortion of scriptural texts, viz. heresy, is due either to ignorance or to instability in faith.

The one, holy, catholic and apostolic Church of God, consists of all the particular holy Churches of God, which being divinely planted, like luxuriant vines throughout the orthodox world, are inseparably united to each other in the unity of the one saving faith in Christ, and in the bond of peace and of the Spirit. There one may meet the highlypraised and most glorious Lord and God and Saviour Jesus Christ who suffered for the salvation of the world.

St. John Chrysostom says: "not even the blood of martyrdom can wash away the sin of schism in the Church". And it is known that the schism between the Eastern and Western Church was caused by the Papal Church. Pope John Paul II himself confessed it in 1995 in his famous encyclical "Orientale Lumen". The magnitude of this sin is obvious to all.

The Pope's claim to primacy of world power, and infallibility, of being a vicar, that is a representantive of Christ on earth, is a fundamental distortion of Christianity. There are probably transgressions in the Orthodox world by individuals, priests, or bishops, but these are rare incidents of individual behavior. These are not a problem of institution. In the

Western Church transgression and sin have been institutionalized. In the latter, if you do not accept the pope with his absolute primacy of authority and infallibility, you are not a Christian, you will not be saved. Here is an institutionalization and dogmatization of sin.

"In things concerning faith there must be no concessions, no waverings" (St Mark of Ephesus). Our holy Fathers used to say, "I shall never reject thee, beloved Orthodoxy, and will not conceal thee, holy tradition, while my spirit dwells in this my body." And our Church in each holy service prays to God the Father: "Return those who have gone astray and join them to Your catholic and apostolic Church."

Therefore, it is a vital necessity for us all to resort to the united Church of the first eight centuries, to the Church that has preserved and does preserve unbroken and unadultarated the apostolic tradition, to the true Church of Christ, so that our Lord's prayer, which He made in behalf of the unity of all christians may be fulfilled, that we all become "one flock" under the Chief-shepherd Christ, who is the head of the Church, His body, *the pillar and ground of the truth.*

It is a consolation to think that within the Western Church itself there are persons who have studied tradition, who see the ecclesiological and dogmatical deviations of Roman Catholic Church and criticize scholastic theology. There are some theologians amid the Western Church who challenge the primacy and the Filioque as well as other innovations of the Roman Catholics and demand a return to the sources of the ancient united Church. These are right-minded people who believe that the surmounting of conflicts between both Churches is possible if they show respect to tradition, so that both Churches, being united, can bear witness together to our rapidly evolving world.

BIBLIOGRAPHY

1. *The History of the Council of Florence,* Boston, 1971.
2. John Romanides, *The Filioque,* Athens.
3. N.Vasiliades, Ὀρθοδοξία καί Παπισμός ἐν διαλόγῳ *(Orthodoxy and Papacy in dialogue),* Athens, 1981.
4. *The Reply of the Orthodox Church to Roman Catholic Overtures on Reunion,* N. York, 1958.
5. G. Metallinos, Τί εἶναι Ὀρθοδοξία; *(What is Orthodoxy?),* Athens, 1980.
6. Vl. Lossky, *The Mystical Theology of the Eastern Church,* James Clarke, London, 1957.
7. Timothy Ware, *The Orthodox Church,* Penguin Books, 1963.
8. Timothy Ware, *The Orthodox Way.*
9. N. Zernov, *Eastern Christendom,* Weindenfeld & Nicolson, London, 1961.
10. Gogol, *Catechism of the Orthodox Church,* Holy Trinity monastery, Jordanville, N.Y. 13361, U.S.A.

11. Khomiakov, *The Church is One*, Holy Trinity monastery, Jordanville, N.Y. 13361, U.S.A.
12. J. Meyendorff, *Byzantine Theology*, Mowbrays, London, 1975.
13. *Orthodox Spirituality*, by a monk of the Eastern Church, London, 1961.
14. Father Sophrony, *His life is mine*, Essex.
15. Methodios Foyas, *Orthodoxy, Roman Catholicism and Anglicanism*, London Oxford University Press, 1972.
16. J. Popovitch, Ὀρθόδοξος Ἐκκλησία καί Οἰκουμενισμός *(Orthodox Church and Ecumenism)*, Thessaloniki, 1974.
17. V. Bakoyannis, *"One Lord, one Faith"*, Patra, 2000.
18. M. Harper, *"The True Light"*, London, 1997.